In This Season

In This Season

Words for the Heart

Todd Nesloney,
LaNesha Tabb,
Tanner Olson,
and Alice Lee

ConnectEDD Publishing
Hanover, Pennsylvania

This publication is available at discount pricing when purchased in quantity for educational purposes, promotions, or fundraisers. For inquiries and details, contact the publisher at
info@connecteddpublishing.com

Published by ConnectEDD Publishing, LLC
Hanover, PA
www.connecteddpublishing.com

Cover Design: Kheila Dunkerly

In This Season: Words for the Heart/Todd Nesloney, Alice Lee, Tanner Olson, and LaNesha Tabb. —1st ed.
Paperback ISBN 979-8-9860690-0-5

Praise for *In This Season*

"*In This Season: Words for the Heart* is filled with treasures that will ignite writers to explore and take risks with their own writing. This book will be a staple in my classroom—through all the seasons of writing in a school year. I have so many favorite lines, but this one stands out: "...let it always be summer in my soul." These chapters will reach so many young writers' souls. Wow! Wow!! Wow!!!"

—Frank Murphy | Author and Educator

"*In This Season* offers readers an opportunity to reflect on what truly matters while providing opportunities for daily doses of inspiration. You'll learn more about fulfillment, belonging, and truth, all while reminding us to consider the components of human capital, like loyalty, health, and happiness."

—Stephen Ventura | founder Advanced Collaborative Solutions, and author of *Achievement Teams: How a Better Approach to PLCs Can Improve Student Outcomes and Teacher Efficacy*

"Hope springs eternal for educators who are lucky enough to find this book and share it with their communities. Halfway through reading it, I literally exhaled and felt stronger and more equipped to lead during and through these uncertain times. You and your teams will be reminded that by reflecting and rejuvenating, you will prevail and be stronger. Together we are on our way."

—Anne Wissinger | Bookelicious Chief Experience Officer, Scholastic Book Fairs Reading Summit Co-Founder

"*In This Season: Words for the Heart* is a beautiful compilation of poetry sure to uplift and support readers of all ages. Honest and raw, written by esteemed educators, it will speak to people in all the different seasons they experience."

—Gaia Cornwall | Author and Illustrator of children's books, including Charlotte Zolotow Honoree, *Jabari Jumps*

"*In This Season* is motivational and thought provoking. It encourages the reader to reflect even on the little things in life because no thought or action is too big nor small; it's just a matter of perspective. It collectively sends the message that we all matter. We can all make a difference, but it has to start somewhere, and that somewhere or someone can be me."

—Edith Moreno | Executive Assistant, M.C. Byrd Wealth Management

"Our lives change rapidly—sometimes by choice, others naturally or by circumstance. No matter where you are and what you go through, though, words can help us navigate difficult times, identify uncertain feelings, and enjoy celebratory moments. *In This Season* brings you these words, and this group of diverse minds have authored a book that can reach your heart on any level through inspiration, guidance, and reflection. You'll finish this book not only looking back on the moments and decisions of your life in a new light, but you'll be ready to move forward onto new adventures and opportunities with transformed focus and perspective."

—Adam Dovico | educator, author, international speaker

"With creativity, art, and opportunities for personal reflection, this resource offers hope when we are feeling wrung out, burnt out, or at the end of our hope tank. *In This Season* gently walks through the seasons of both Creation and the human experience, connecting us to rhythms that restore and refresh us and remind us we are not far from God and those who love us. This text is particularly useful for the transitions of life—ones that surprise us, and ones more expected—inviting us to take time for processing in the middle of change."

—Heidi Goehmann | LCSW

"*In This Season: Words for the Heart* was thoughtfully put together. Reading through the writing, poems, and essays felt like sitting down with a familiar friend who always knows the right thing to say even when it's hard to hear. *'You are worthy. You deserve. You are needed because you are literally you. Walk into every room, even the one where NO ONE looks like you and you take all the space you need.'* This quote will sit with me for a while."

—Naomi O'Brien | Educator, Author, National Speaker

"*In This Season: Words for the Heart*, perfectly describes all the seasons we seem to go through in life. The good, the bad, the overwhelming, and the times when you just want to give up. The stories and poems in this book help you see you that no matter what life throws at you, you are not alone, and you will make it through. A beautiful reminder that there is always hope."

—Jocelyn White | Chiropractic Assistant, Bartay Chiropractic

"Throughout *In This Season*, the authors encourage you to be an active participant as you reflect on the words and engage in the exercises on the pages. The invitation is offered to dig deep and act on your feelings. You'll read with an anticipation to participate. *In This Season* reminds you that you were created with a hope and a purpose!"

—Nancy Fritz | retired educator and administrator

Dedication

To those who need a word to carry with them today.
This is for you.

Table of Contents

Introduction

For those who feel stuck or behind…
For those who feel lost in their own thoughts…
For those who are going through the motions…
For those who wonder how you'll make it through another day…
For those who ache to express how they feel…
For those who are wanting to be seen…
For those who just need a vacation…

This is for you.

The book you are holding is a collection of writings, poems, and essays from four different authors from four different areas of the United States. In our own unique ways we are educators, creators, and helpers. One thing the four of us have in common is that we have hope.

Our reason for creating this book is that we long to share with you that hope is still alive and hope is for you.

It goes without saying, but life is often heavy and full of unknowns. Each of us has endured the cold of winter, the growth of spring, the light of summer, and the change of fall. We have weathered storm after storm and season after season, but by grace we are still here.

As tomorrow arrives may these pages invite you to reflect on how far you've come and where you dream of going. Sit with the words we plucked and pulled from our hearts. Let this book meet you where you are and encourage you to step into what is to come with hope.

PART I

Spring

Spring. The season signifying birth and life from the
cold winter. The time of renewed hope, envisioned future,
blossoming beginnings. The season in which we slowly start
trading our winter coats and boots for lighter jackets
and longer strolls outdoors. Refresh and rejuvenate
into a spring brimming with possibility.

BLOOMING

To bloom is to grow.

To begin again.

To recover.

To start fresh.

To explore.

We bloom in private.

We can bloom in several different ways all at the same time.

We might bloom while something else is dying.

Blooming signifies something new.

A new season, a change.

Welcome the bloom.

We all need to grow, to bloom into new and improved versions of ourselves.

Each new day is in itself a new opportunity to bloom.

To bloom is to hope.

To bloom is to reconstruct.

GROWTH

Growth looks like ...
Asking for forgiveness.
Saying I'm sorry.
Resting from work.
Admitting your need for help.
Holding onto hope when life feels heavy.
Believing you are who God says you are.
Celebrating how far you've come.
Bringing forward anxious thoughts and fears.
Listening instead of interrupting.
Changing what isn't working.
Telling others you don't know.
Reminding yourself you are loved regardless of your performance.
Pausing with the silence.
Letting go of what needs to go.
Doing the hard thing.
And I've still got a lot of growing to do.
So, here we grow.
It is the tiny changes of today that will create a better tomorrow.

TRUTH

There is truth. And there is sharing truth, shedding light on truth, speaking truth.

But when truth is revealed, or shared, or spoken, how do we communicate truth?

When truth conflicts, when truth aggravates, when truth upheaves, when one is right and another is wrong, how is this truth revealed? Does it speak through curt statements, biting words, and unnecessarily bitter actions? Or is it said with humility, with understanding, with empathy?

Those who loudly claim, "Do as I say!" and "See what I'm doing?!" yet have little patience, demonstrate little reflection on *how* their truth communicates to others. What does truth do in these moments?

No. I will not do as you say, nor do as you do because your actions and words conflict and contradict.

No. I will resist passively and silently as your fear-mongering ways have an unfortunate impact in my life.

So YES. I will practice my own sense of humility, my own sense of preservation for the time being.

Speak truth with love. Speak truth with peace. Speak truth with patience. Speak truth with time.

And one day, when there is a crossroad between delivering truth mired in hurt and pain, may you be approached with humility. May you be given the benefit of the doubt. May you be met with grace. And may you be treated with undeserved compassion.

May we all come to understand and know truth, to be set free, and to have peace abound.

BE

HAPPY
CREATIVE
KIND
AUTHENTIC
COOL
ADVENTUROUS
BOLD
TRUE
HUMBLE
STRONG
·HONEST
·GENTLE LOYAL
PATIENT
PERSISETENT
DIFFERENT
VISIONARY
THANKFUL
RESOURCEFULL
UNSTOPPABLE
GENEROUS
A FRIEND
·MOTIVATIONAL
LEGENDARY ·ACCEPTING·

AWESOME
CHEERFUL ·CARING
SMART
BRAVE
IMAGINITIVE ·NICE
KINDHEARTED
FORGIVING
TRUSTWORTHY
DARING·
GRATEFUL SUPPORTIVE WISE
INSPIRATIONAL

YOU.

These days I am reminding myself to remain where I am and simply inhale and exhale.

I haven't forgotten how to breathe, but some days I need a reminder to breathe.

I often write how life is heavy (because it is) and hard (because it is).

And amidst the worry and fear, I forget to breathe and be.

So here I am.

Learning again to breathe and be.

Breathing is a beautiful reminder that I am here.

Here where everything is far from perfect, but still beautiful.

Sometimes I have to tilt my head or take a step back to see the beauty, but it's there.

It is.

And sometimes I have to remind myself that it's going to be ok.

It may not feel like it today, but it's going to be ok.

As I inhale and exhale, I slow down and remind myself of the few things I know to be true.

I don't have to worry.

I don't need to overthink every little thing.

I don't have to run from fear.

Instead, I can simply breathe and be.
No longer do I need to fixate on what was or what is or what will be.
I can just breathe and be.

Inhale.

Exhale.

Inhale.

Exhale.

Breathe and be.

FORWARD

I'm not sure what comes next.
Maybe it's good news
Or maybe it's not-so-good news.
For all I do not know
I know you've made it this far
through the uncertain,
through the unknown,
through the unexpected,
and maybe
that's the reminder you need
to keep on going forward.

Keep on going forward.

FUTURE

When it seems like everyone is moving ahead
Faster and higher
Gaining more, reaching further
And I'm watching from where I stand
Toiling and grinding away with where I've been, from what I know
Feeling uneasy, but comfortable

Am I supposed to move, too?
Do I stay or do I go?

The mixed messages of don't get too comfortable,
Do what you know...
This space is fulfilling...

Yet I wonder...

What would happen if a risk were taken?
A step was pondered outside the familiar?
Will I face acceptance?
Rejection?

What does tomorrow look like?

And there's no way to tell what the future will hold,
But the steps we take today, the choices we make today,
Lead to a tomorrow that will be different from today and yesterday.

What do you imagine for your tomorrows?
What do you dream for your future?
A new job? Home? Community?
A refreshed sense of being?
Freedom from bitterness?
Encountering new joy and adventure?

What can you do today to inch or catapult into the hopes for tomorrow?

There is something powerful in the physical act of writing, typing, and verbally proclaiming what it is you want, what you hope.

Write it out.
Journal or scribble it somewhere.
Map it.
Share it.
Tell a friend.
Dream together, journey together.

May our tomorrows and futures be bright, fulfilling, and restorative.
May others be positively impacted because of your choices today.

REFLECTION

Hold still for a moment as today comes to a close.

Become aware of the ups and downs since the sun first rose.

Meet the end of the day with an honest exhale.

Here are a few questions to reflect on as today becomes yesterday:

What went well today?

What did you feel today?

What brought you the most life today?

What drained you today?

Who helped you make it through another day?

What is your hope for tomorrow?

When tomorrow arrives, how will you greet it?

What is something you need to remember when tomorrow begins to weigh heavy?

HOPE

Hope /hōp/ (noun)

- a feeling of expectation and desire for a certain thing to happen
- a person or thing that may help or save someone
- grounds for believing that something good might happen

Hope holds us together. It allows us to push through and keep trying.

What do you hope for?

No, really. Stop reading these words and take a minute to think about it. Like really think about.

Ok, did you think? Now, stop reading again and write your hopes down. Get it out of your head.

Got it written down? Ok, when you look at the list of things you hope for, how do you feel?

Do those hopes feel attainable? Possible? Crazy?

Maybe you hope....

- you or someone you love will be healed
- for that dream house to come on the market
- you get the call back for the interview you just finished

- there is enough money in your bank account to pay for groceries this week
- that they notice you
- this pregnancy makes it to term
- that they have your size at the store
- the restaurant actually gets your order right this time
- you make it to the gas station because your low fuel light has been on for two days
- the copy machine isn't broken
- the test results are different this time
- the series finale doesn't disappoint

What do you hope for?

We can't allow others to tell us that our hopes are silly.

They're ours.

Hope is a feeling. A person. A thing. A belief.

It's one of those. It's all of those. It's what holds us together.

But what about when our hope leads to disappointment? Do we stop hoping?

We can't stop hoping.

Hope is healing, it is powerful, it keeps us moving forward.

What do you hope for? Don't keep it in. Share it.

PART II

Summer

These days the light remains a little while longer. We enjoy the beautiful gifts of Spring as we anticipate the falling leaves and changes of Autumn. But for now, we hold onto what is. We celebrate the warmth, gather together around the campfire or below the late evening stars. In this, we are reminded that beauty is for us. And I cannot help but think: let it always be summer in my soul.

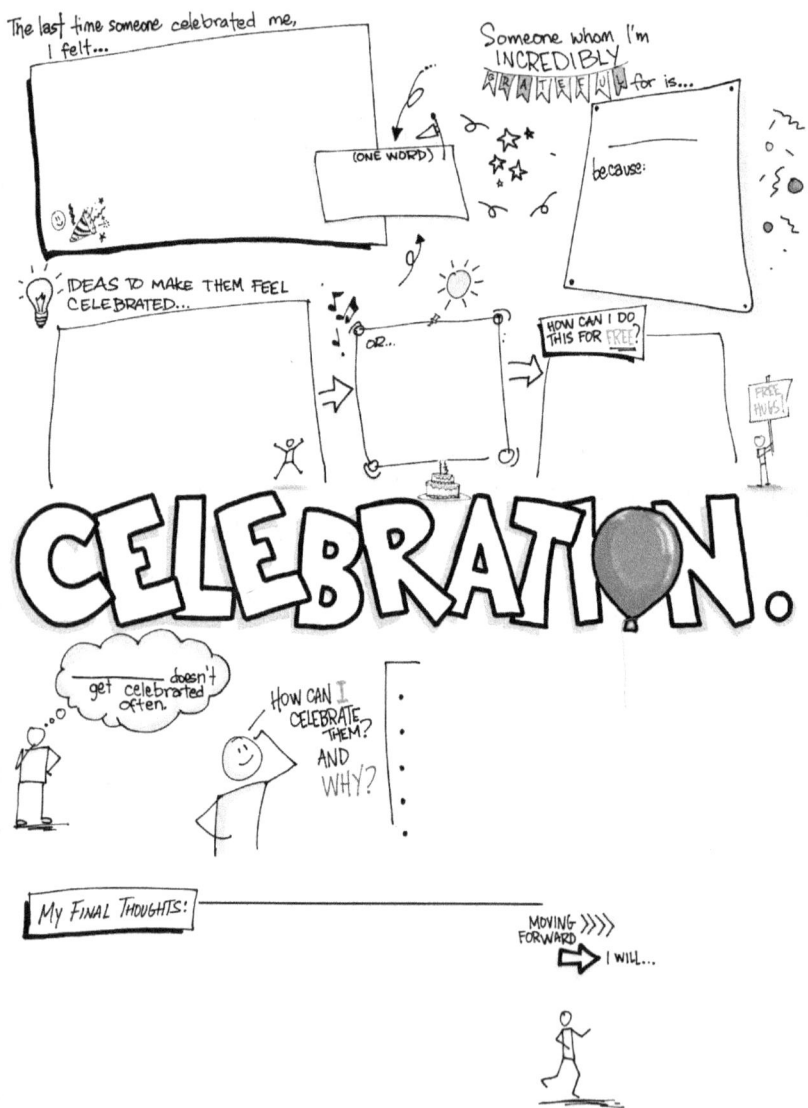

The last time someone celebrated me, I felt...

(ONE WORD)

Someone whom I'm INCREDIBLY GRATEFUL for is...

because:

IDEAS TO MAKE THEM FEEL CELEBRATED...

OR...

HOW CAN I DO THIS FOR FREE?

FREE HUGS!

CELEBRATION.

doesn't get celebrated often.

HOW CAN I CELEBRATE THEM? AND WHY?

My FINAL THOUGHTS:

MOVING FORWARD
I WILL...

CELEBRATION

Deep down everyone loves to be celebrated. We all want to feel seen, valued, and important.

But rather than talk about celebration, sometimes it's just as important to reflect.

So let's reflect.

When was the last time someone celebrated you? Below, write down from start to finish (yes, write in this book!) what happened and then identify one word that you felt deep inside yourself after reflecting on the celebration.

Who is someone in your life right now that you are incredibly grateful for? Write below about what makes them so important to you?

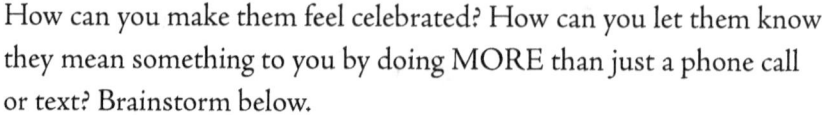

How can you make them feel celebrated? How can you let them know they mean something to you by doing MORE than just a phone call or text? Brainstorm below.

Now that you've brainstormed, celebrations don't have to cost ANY money. How can you take your ideas above and do something FREE?

Now for the tough part. Think about someone in your life (personal or professional) who probably doesn't get celebrated often. Maybe they're quiet and blend into the background. Maybe they are often viewed as bitter. How can YOU celebrate them? But more importantly WHY should you celebrate them? Share your thoughts below.

Many think of celebration as full of so much joy. But the reflection piece before this one may have been difficult for you. Why do you think it's difficult to celebrate those who aren't always celebrated? If everyone deserves to feel valued, don't they deserve to be celebrated, too? Why should you be leading the charge in that?

Now that you've reflected, thinking about how celebrations make you and others feel, what will you do differently moving forward?

FUN

Am I fun?
Did I forget how to have fun?
I think I'm fun… aren't I?
Yeah, I'm fun.
I have fun…yeah.
Wait, how are we **defining** fun?
Well, I just tried to define "fun" so that might make me definitely *not* fun.
I have some friends, I laugh…
But do I really have enough fun?
Sometimes fun can feel foreboding.
Like, if I allow myself some "fun" will I just be setting myself up to be devastated when the other shoe drops?
Do I have to keep fun at bay just in case?

Search: How to have fun (drop down google search)

- How to have fun in **life**
- How to have fun in life again
- How to have fun in marriage
- How to have fun in life without friends
- How to have fun in even if you're lonely
- How to have fun in a relationship
- How to have fun at work
- How to have fun and make friends
- How to have fun with my kids

🔍 How to have fun when you're tired

🔍 How to have fun when you just like books and coffee

🔍 How to have fun without eating or drinking

🔍 How to have fun while working at the same time

🔍 How to have fun at school

🔍 _____

I may have possibly forgotten how to have real fun. That may be true.
But I know that I need it.
I'm worthy of fun.
I deserve fun.
You do, too.

How are you feeling about fun? Write. Share. Then, have some.

JOY

My hand scribbles across the page...

"There is joy in this."

And I wondered, is this true?

My hand has written many things and smeared even more.

My soul has written books and novels, but the right hand of my over-thinking mind has deleted every single one of them.

But maybe these five words will remain.

There is joy in this.

It sounded true in my mouth, but it felt like a lie to my eyes.

I've been staring deep into those five words on a single line like they're the sunset ending the day, dipping into the sea and without the sunlight it's hard to see, but still, there is joy in this.

Or at least I'm beginning to see with the growing and groaning light of the sunrise that these five words are true, despite the darkness and moments of feeling broken and blue.

Despite the wondering and sadness and sentences you just don't quite know how to end...

There is joy in this.

Joy is defined in many ways by many different writers and thinkers.

I don't have a great definition, but may I offer this:

Joy is kind, always inviting other feelings to join.

Often joy will be accompanied by pain and anger and fear and sadness.

Today, and every day, you are allowed to feel more than one thing at once.

Joy and pain.
Joy and sadness.
Joy and fear.
Joy and _____.

There is joy in this.
Even in this.

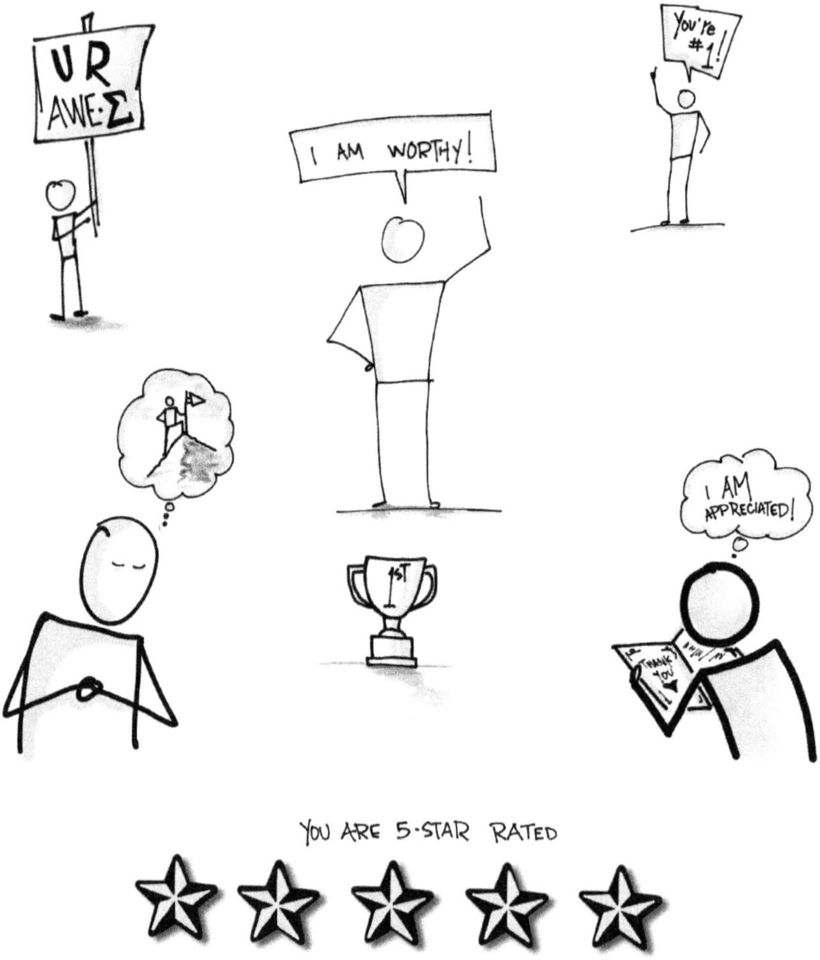

DESERVING

When I think about what I "deserve" it can stop me dead in my tracks.

Because I begin to wonder, what do I deserve? Do I deserve...

> to be happy?
> my job?
> to be loved?
> good things to happen to me?
> my spouse?
> success?

And I can lose myself in how wild my thoughts will take off. It feels like I hike down a trail into a forest only to get lost when I wander off the path of what I know to be true.

Because the reality is, I am deserving. And yes, YOU are deserving.

The situation we find ourselves in at this very moment is exactly where we were supposed to be.

The trials, the joys, the success, the failure, the pain, the struggle. All of it matters.

Do you deserve to be loved? Yes.

Do you deserve to be happy? Yes.

Do you deserve to have a job where you are valued and appreciated?
Yes.

Do you deserve to feel successful? Yes.

But sometimes this can definitely be easier said than done. So on the
days when I don't feel like I am worthy, or that I deserve what I've
been given, or even that I deserve great things at all here's what I do....

First, I sit in that moment, close my eyes and breathe. Just the simple
act of blocking everything out and breathing for one minute can some
days help bring what matters back into focus.

If that doesn't work—because let's be real, it doesn't always work—then
I write down how I'm feeling. I get it out of my head and don't let it
take root and lead me into the wilderness. I can't tell you how many
times I've felt freed by the simple act of allowing my thoughts to
become words on paper.

And finally, I ground myself in what I know to be reality. This was
a great skill I learned in therapy (yes, therapy isn't for just when you
have a problem. But that's another chapter for another day). In my
good moments, I know what the reality is. I know I was created for a
purpose. I know I am fearfully and wonderfully made. I know I hold
immeasurable worth. Regardless of how I feel in the moment, the
reality can sometimes be different and I need to reground myself.

So, what DO you deserve? Make a list. Share it with a friend. Don't
allow your own insecurities or doubts to stop you.

CONFIDENCE

Building your own table—and the chairs, too.

You are worthy. You deserve. You are needed because you are literally you.

Walk into every room, even the one where NO ONE looks like you and you take all the space you need. You're not an imposter; you are an expert because your lived experiences combined with the knowledge you've acquired said so.

And, imposter syndrome is the most selfish. It's raggedy. Just walking around here robbing folks of the gifts that you have to give. Don't negotiate with terrorists like this.

I know, some of us feel entitled to the table. Don't, please. It's played out.

I mean, imagine believing that you and a select few are the only people worthy of sitting at the table. You're missing out, friend. Dopeness abounds.

Some of us have spent our time gathering the tools needed to begin construction on our own tables because we've been rejected by one table too many. Good.

Grab your hammer of hope, your tape measure of tenacity, and your nails of "Oh no, you didn't…"

And get to work.

TOGETHER

We can love.
We can hope.
We can continue.

And somehow, we will.
We will take the broken pieces and together become whole.
We will take steps forward with faith for each other.
We will take the dreams of our neighbors and carry them into reality.
We will take today and step with peace into tomorrow.

For what stands before us is the glow of the rising sun.
We will come out of the shadows victorious.
We will come into the light side-by-side and stand together on the
other side.
Below the beams of beauty we will move forward.

For even when life feels far from right, we will always have the light.

Today, we can love.
We can hope.
We can continue.

Together we can.
Together we will.

HONESTY

You ever have that friend/colleague/acquaintance who says something totally rude or inappropriate and follows it with "I was just being honest."

Insert angry face emoji.

That's how I feel when I hear it.

But what is honesty? When you look at the etymology of the word "honesty" it comes from the Latin *honestas* which means "honor, respectable".

When we're honest with others do, we do it in a way that brings honor? Are we respectable in our honesty?

I can think of many instances when I have not been respectable. When my honesty hurt someone instead of helped.

Does that mean our honesty will always heal instead of hurt? Not necessarily. Sometimes when you are honest with someone it is hard. It is painful.

But I remember the simple fact that we must have people in our lives who are honest enough with us to say...
- No
- You need to apologize

- That was inappropriate
- It's not quite time for that idea yet
- You need to take a step back

But when those in our lives share that honesty, we only truly hear it when it comes from a place of love. An honorable place. A respectable place. The heart.

Some will hide behind "honesty" as an excuse to belittle, demean, and "just share the truth." But when you aren't honorable or respectable while being "honest," by definition you literally aren't even being honest. You're just being a jerk.

Yeah, I said it.

We all need those who will be honest with us.
We all need to be honest with others.
But in the end, it must come from a place of love if we expect our honesty to lead to change.

Are you ready to be honest?

HELP

As children, we have no problem asking for help.

Can you help me tie my shoe?
Can you hand me that?
Will you carry me?

Yet at some point we stop asking for help. Maybe it's us trying to feel more independent. But it's probably our insecurities.

Sometimes we wonder if we'll be judged. Will it make us look weak? Will people think we're incapable of doing difficult things? Will I be embarrassed?

When you reflect on your own experiences, what comes to mind as something that has been tough lately that you probably should have asked for help and didn't?

Sometimes the help we need to ask for involves people around us that we know.

Asking a family member to pick up our child from school because our meeting is running late.
Asking a co-worker to help us figure out the new computer program.
Asking for an extension.
Asking someone to help you change your tire.
Asking for help in carrying the heavy box.

Then again, sometimes the help we must seek comes from someone who is a professional in a particular field.

It can be as simple as calling Apple or the Geek Squad at Best Buy and asking them for help in fixing your computer. Or calling the kid down the street to mow your lawn.

But maybe it's asking for help that goes a little deeper.

Maybe it's scheduling an appointment with your primary care physician because your anxiety or depression is out of control and you're ready to seek help.

Maybe it's finding a therapist you can talk to that will help you verbalize what's in your head or work through a concern.

For some strange reason we believe that when we don't ask for help, we're actually showing strength.

But when I reflect on the many times I didn't ask for help, and should have, it never made me look stronger. Instead, I burnt out quicker, broke down faster, and made more mistakes than I needed to.

Ask for help. There is always more strength in vulnerability.

PART III

Autumn

The shifting of each season makes itself known with changes in temperature and mood. Blazing hot days and feelings can morph into cool collections of thought. Autumn is for sharing. Autumn is gifted with gratitude and growth. Pull out your pumpkin-spiced everything and receive the words that will spark grace, forgiveness, and belonging.

REST

My alarm cuts the silence and lights up the room at 6:00 a.m.
I walk the dog, make breakfast, do some reading, and then sit down at my desk.
Ten tabs are still open from the day before.
A handful of new emails bounce in my inbox waiting to be replied to or deleted or left alone until I have had enough coffee in my system to think of a coherent response.
I add a few more things to my already long to-do list.
I take a sip of coffee and whisper to myself those two damaging words:
Let's grind.

Okay, I don't actually say that.
That would be weird.

All of this to say, we've worshiped working and have ignored the beauty of rest.

Here are a few things I know about *rest*:
Rest is holy.
Rest is vital.
Rest sustains.
Last year, my friend Barrett shared with me a few words that have changed how I view *rest*. He said, "We **work from *rest*, we don't *rest* from work."**
We begin with *rest*.
This goes against everything I have ever known.

Like Rihanna, all I wanted to do was work, work, work, work, not rest.

There is always a list of things to do.
There is always something to write or clean or fix.
There is always someone to call or text or meet up with.
There is always something to do, but what if *rest* is where we begin?

Slowly I've been learning that *resting* is not wasted time, but it is using our time wisely.
And it is *rest* that will allow me to not only work, but (hopefully) do better work.

It's almost as if...
I need to step away in order to come back.
I need to slow down to move forward.
I need to sit back so I can prepare to lean in and move forward.
I need to shut it off and *rest* before I work.

I've heard that to *rest* is to *trust.*
Moving forward I plan to begin with *rest*, trusting that the rest will follow.

FAMILY:

WORK:

PERSONAL:

HOME:

WHAT or WHO ARE YOU GRATEFUL FOR?

MY GRATITUDE QUILT

GRATITUDE

In the height of joy, at the peaks of elation, there is gratitude.
When there is an extra garlic sauce thrown into the bag of freshly
baked pita bread, there is gratitude.
When the dog rambunctiously shakes his tail and twirls in dizzying
circles upon your arrival home, there is gratitude.
When a friend leaves a Post-it note to say they are thankful for you,
there is gratitude.

Through the mundaneness of life, we express gratitude for the stabil-
ity, for the quiet, predictable ebb and flow of events.
There is gratitude in that we woke to a new day, a quiet glistening
through the windows.
A gentle, "Good morning."
There is gratitude in the simple moments of the day.

In the challenging times and moments,
when chaos consumes our thoughts
preventing us
from practicing gratitude,
from reminiscing the small glimpses of good and giving thanks…
In these moments,
when our spirits are downtrodden, beaten, exhausted from just
being…
In these moments when we struggle for peace, for quiet, for stillness,
These moments of pain and confusion,
when the cavern seems so deep and dark and perilous,
May there be a quickening in our spirits to remember–

That there is hope.
There is purpose.
There will be a better day.
There will be restoration.
There will be another moment for gratitude.

Rehearse and remember the stories of the moments of gratitude, of laughter, of levity.

Take a moment to utter a breath of "thank you."
Through gritted teeth or shouts of joy, "Thank you. I am grateful."
Say it until a thought or memory bubbles back to the surface of something that made your heart warm, happy, proud, safe.

What is one thing that brought me joy, big or small, today?
Who am I thankful for today?
Where is that place I like to go that makes me smile?
What is your favorite flavor of ice cream?

Friends, I wish you well and hope that your day will have at least one moment of goodness, for which you are grateful.

BELONG

When you read the word "belong", where does your mind begin to drift? What emotions start to bubble to the surface?

I believe inside each of us is a deep longing to belong. A need to be wanted.

But what does it mean to belong?

Is belonging....

- Knowing there will always be a seat at the table waiting for you?
- Knowing that when you make that call, the person on the other end will smile as they answer the phone?
- When you speak up, others listen?
- Feeling like you can even speak at all?
- Realizing when they ask, "How are you?" that they really mean it?

What is belonging?

I find that we can all define it differently.

If you're anything like me, you can find yourself feeling left out at one point or another. Heck, you may be reading this right now and wondering where you belong. Who cares? Why bother?

You can watch as you scroll through social media, overhear dinner conversations, watch the television shows, and attend the events where you begin to wonder when you will fit in like all the rest seem to do so effortlessly.

When will you get that invitation?
When will they ask you?
When will you feel like you're needed?

The reality is that we stand in our way more than anything else.

Wait, what? How?

- We create false scenarios in our heads.
- We allow social media to convince us that the joy on the faces is the entire story (when we all know it isn't).
- We make excuses.
- We hide away.
- We try to change ourselves to fit in.

Yep, I'm talking to myself, too. Every day.

But today, why don't we stop? Let's stop comparing, stop sulking, stop hiding.

Embrace what makes us who we are. Seek out our people. Embrace our uniqueness. Be reminded that we aren't alone. That there's so many of us out there who want to belong, too.

We're all just waiting to be asked.

Why not stop waiting, and instead ask someone else to join us at our table.

It always starts with one.

TIME

If ever there was a topic to get deep with, it's time.

What a complex concept.

There's never enough.

It goes so quickly.

It seemingly never ends.

It is spent.

It is saved.

It is needed.

It is desired.

It is marked in seasons and accomplishments.

We try to get it back.

It exists in our memories.

It awaits us in the future.

So how strange is it that...time, which we seem to never have,

Is endless?

It's the thing that we want to give more than anything

But it's also the hardest thing to part with.

We plan to do all of the things when we have the time.

The problem is the fact that doing the things takes most of the time.

Time is so precious, so fleeting.

How can we honor the gift of time?

How do we define "time well spent?"

People have written theories about time.

Einstein said that time is relative—the at which time passes depends on your frame of reference.

Aristotle said that time is not a kind of change, but that it is something dependent on change.
Some say it's cyclical, linear and chaotic.
I'd like to write a theory of my own.
My theory is that time is tempestuous.
It's relentless and vast—uncomfortably so.
How do you wrap your mind around what was and is to come?
How do you make the best of the time you are given?
Take some time to think about it.

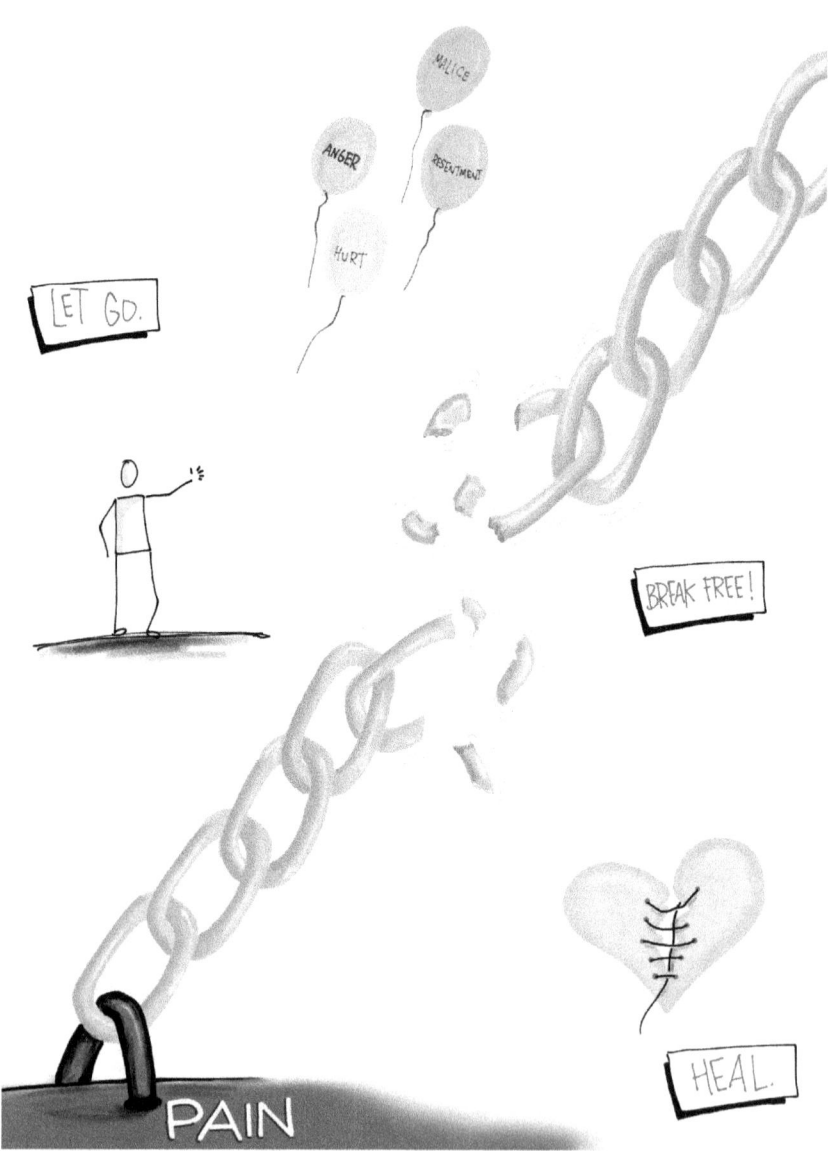

FORGIVENESS

When someone hurts us, forgiveness is probably the last thing on our minds. Instead, we probably have a variety of thoughts that run wild. Thoughts like….

F - From the moment it happened I felt frustrated, upset, and most of all annoyed with myself that I allowed it to happen to me again.

O - Others have talked about forgiveness or revenge. It seems like those are the only two options. Get back at the person or pretend like it never happened.

R - Reality is that I'm not quite sure what will make the pain go away. Part of me doesn't want to forgive because I know I'll never be able to forget that it happened.

G - God reminds me in Romans that revenge will never fill the hole; it will never make me truly feel better. That I should be honorable. But what does that mean?

I - Instead I hold on. I hold onto the pain. I avoid the person. I consider retaliation. I wonder, "Why me?"

V - Validation. I want someone to tell me it's ok to feel this way. I want someone to give me permission to sulk or retaliate. Or maybe I just need someone to tell me to move on.

E - Everyone knows, though: that never works. You can run from your pain, but it will always catch up to you.

N - No one understands what I'm feeling, though. At least that's what I tell myself. No one....but maybe....

E - Ears were created to listen. Why do I keep assuming no one wants to listen to me? To help me? I must share my story. I must begin to release this inside me.

S - Somehow, I've convinced myself that forgiveness is all about me giving the person who hurt me a free pass. That I must forget to forgive. But that's not really true, is it?

S - Sabotage. That's what the enemy does. Instead, I'm reminded that when I choose forgiveness over revenge or holding onto the pain..... when I truly lean into forgiving someone.....I end up freeing myself more than the other. Only I can choose forgiveness. I'm ready to be free.

....FORGIVENESS...

Forgiveness.

Truthfully, this is something I thought I did well.
When an offense is committed, a mistake has been made, and an "I'm sorry" is uttered, forgiveness ensues.

But as the years have passed, I realized, maybe, with some hurts and some pains, recent or past, forgiveness is something I'm working through.

A trust that I thought I had, a trust shared, a relationship that I thought was mutual and symbiotic...only to realize that it was an unbalanced seesaw, where one was grounded in the belief that there was mutuality, while the other was floating in false flattery.

Psychologists state that the act of forgiveness is a deliberate, intentional, and conscious decision to *release* the feelings of hurt towards someone, a group, a memory. Regardless of whether it is deserving. Regardless of whether an apology is made. Regardless.

It is like grace—a favor that is undeserved, unmerited, and completely free.

Forgiveness is powerful. And it resides within you. Within me.
And what's even more powerful about forgiveness, is that it's really for you. It's for you to intentionally choose to release someone, thing, event from *your* pain.

It's not to say to forget. Don't forget.
But release the vengeance. Release the vindictiveness. Release the
resentment.

Set. Myself. Free.

So I'm working on forgiving, this act of forgiveness.
To give my spirit reprieve from the hurt,
To give my heart the peace it deserves and needs,
And to release the offender from taking any more space than was ever
necessary in my mind, time, feelings, and thoughts.

I pray to know peace, grace, and release.
And I pray this for you.

Onward and forward with lightness in our steps.

SHARING

We live in the age of sharing as a rule.

We used to joke about not eating or drinking until we could snap a picture to share online, but now it's barely even a joke.

There's a meme out there that encourages people to "take a beach vacation without sharing any pictures" to which the reply reads "I'm not about to be relaxing on the beach without letting haters know!"

It's funny, but it's also kind of true for a lot of us.

We've become conditioned to expect a certain level of sharing.

And then there's the literal sense of the word. Especially when we were little.

Share!

Be nice, and share!

Oh, look how nicely you two are sharing.

At first glance, it's like, "Yes! Of course sharing is good."

Necessary.

Expected.

But then you watch a child happily playing with a toy on their own.

Another child comes over and proceeds to take that toy from the child who was perfectly happy.

So, because another child simply wanted the toy, the first child is automatically expected to share? Why, though?

Is that life? Share or else?

Whether you are sharing your toys or your deepest thoughts, it's a special privilege to share and be shared with in return.

It's not owed.

Sharing is a sign of trust.

It's the allocation of treasures.

It's the careful and curated distribution and dividing of…ourselves.

The partaking of precious moments.

The splitting of special scenes that we hold dear.

It's holding out the other half of the headphone to share a song.

We share when we feel safe.

Do you feel safe? Right now…in this setting you find yourself in.

If you feel comfortable…
         share.

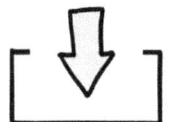

RECEIVE

I bet you're probably a little like me.

Ok yes, I am making a pretty big assumption here, but I'm very comfortable in believing I'm right.

How are you like me?

You probably have a very hard time receiving.

Receiving?

Yes, receiving.

If I were to stand in front of a room filled with people, grab the mic, and then proceed to tell them how absolutely incredible you are, how would you feel?

Would you beam with joy? Nod your head in agreement? Bask in the compliments?

Or would you find yourself disagreeing, trying to hide your face, or struggling to believe the words that I was saying about you?

You see, as humans, we suck at receiving good things. More often than not we will sabotage those good moments.

But why?

Sometimes it's our own insecurities. Sometimes we truly don't believe those good things were meant for us. Sometimes we don't feel *deserving*.

So how do we get better at receiving? How do we allow those moments to wash over and seep into us?

Give. That's the first step.

When you give those moments of joy, celebration, affirmation to others you get to experience how good it feels to give. You have that euphoria take over. In that moment, hold onto that feeling. Because when someone gives to you, remind yourself to receive it in the same way.

Accept.

Accept that when others celebrate or uplift you that is how THEY feel. You can't tell someone how to feel or what they're feeling is wrong. If they took the time to build you up, then what they're saying is their truth. So accept that truth.

Discover.

Take the time to really dive into and discover what is holding you back from receiving the goodness someone is sending your way. When you can determine the cause of your defiance, then you can begin to work through it.

You've probably experienced that moment when you've given some-one a gift and you could tell they didn't love it, and you were probably crushed. Or is that just me?

Because you see, when we do allow ourselves to receive, we don't only feel the goodness sent by someone else, but we also validate the other person. We let them know we appreciate the effort they made to give.

Today you can stop holding yourself hostage by your insecurities and, instead, receive what others have to give.

GRIEF

Who is in charge of grief–because I'd like to talk to the manager.

I'd like to formally file a complaint about grief.

The grief who leaves a love-shaped hole in our lives.

The grief who chokes us up in the middle of the night.

The grief who makes our eyes sting at the sight of happiness because **they** are no longer here.

The grief who rehearses the most devastating moments of our lives until it's an absolutely flawless performance.

The grief who leaves us to replay the memories, the messages, the songs.

The grief who makes itself at home, an unwanted houseguest for far too long.

The grief who leaves us lonely.

The grief who sends friend requests to anxiety (and we know anxiety is never one to miss a party).

Oh—and the grief who decides to show up in different ways for different people who are both equally hurting but unable to understand each other's pain. *That's rude.*

Do you have any redeeming qualities, grief? I mean, **good GRIEF.**

Are you supposed to redeem yourself because we have been made stronger by your presence?

Is your presence supposed to give us insights that we would not otherwise understand?

Is it that gratitude for things that remain is made stronger through the lens of grief?

I don't know.

I don't think I can know until you ease up a bit.

Please, ease up.

I want to grow from you, grief.

I need to grow, grief.

GRACE

Did you get my email? Make sure you check emails before you come in. Don't forget to add your data to our team document. You had a customer complaint, come see me. Collect the fundraiser money, count it, and turn it in please. You can work your kid's basketball game concession stand tonight, right? Right? Why didn't your student do well on this test? Can you head up the committee for this new initiative? This flyer needs to be redone. You will need to use your lunch break for that. We don't have any funding for that, but you can write a grant. You aren't as positive as you usually are. Have you turned in your report–the office needs those immediately. Are you going to be out again? So when you're out like, how unavailable will you be? Can you still get your numbers in? We are having a company canned food drive. Be sure to promote it. Collect the cans. We need you to run the staff meeting today. Send out the agenda. Your evaluation is tomorrow. Did you collect any box tops this week? None? You know your school needs the funding. Maybe create a flyer to send home! Why are you stressed? Self care. Self care. Self care. Oh, you didn't pack lunch today? You didn't have time? Gosh, maybe you can prioritize your time better...are you using your time wisely? Ordering takeout again? Yikes. Staff costume contest! Can't wait to see all of your costumes! Fun! Oh, the copier is down. Try to lower your paper usage, please. See me if you'd like to use the color printer, that has to be approved. I'm home! How was your day? I'm not sure what's for dinner. I'll start on that now. You need help with homework? One second, my phone is ringing. Hey, friend; sorry I've been so MIA. I know you're proba-bly disappointed, but I've been a little busy. Wait…it's *ok?* You're not upset? I should breathe? I should slow down?

I should give myself some…*grace?*

PART IV

Winter

Each season has its own set of emotions and memories attached
to it. But Winter seems to be the season when grief, loss, and struggle
is felt the most. Maybe it's a mix of the often-dreary weather and the
season of holiday events. Maybe it's all in our heads. In the following
pages you'll find reminders that you're never alone, that grief is not
a bad word, hope is tangible, and grace is necessary. So put on your
heavy coat, grab a cup of hot cocoa, and join us in Winter.

MAYBE

Maybe it's a season of holding on or letting go.

Maybe it's a season of slowing down or pushing forward.

Maybe it's a season of leaning in or stepping back.

Maybe it's a season of questions or answers or somewhere in between.

However this season finds you, may this be your reminder:
Grace has been with you and will always be before you.

REMEMBER

Remember when you felt the most cared for.
Remember when you got exactly what you needed.
Remember when you were truly proud of yourself.

Remember how you show up best for yourself.
Remember how you show up best for others.
Remember how valuable you are.

Remember why you are on this earth.
Remember why you matter.
Remember why you are worthy of every good thing.

Remember to take up space.
Remember to speak up.
Remember to listen and learn, always.

Remember.

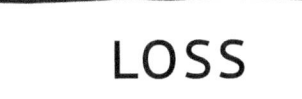

LOSS

I called you today. Dialed the number I've had memorized since I was 11. It went straight to voicemail, as it does every time.

I miss you.

While shopping, a woman walked by and was wearing the same perfume you wore every day, rain or shine, sitting at home or going out. It stopped me in my tracks.

I miss you.

My son smiled at me this morning. A big, toothy, wide smile. The moment he did, I saw you in that smile. It's just like yours.

I miss you.

I drove by your favorite restaurant last night. I still can't go inside. Some days I consider taking a different path so I don't have to see it.

I miss you.

A memory of us crossed my mind at lunch, and you know what? For the first time since I lost you, I didn't cry. I smiled. Small, but it's a start.

I miss you.

I tried cooking one of your recipes that I found hidden away. It didn't even come close to tasting like what you would cook us, but it still made me feel like you were there.

I miss you.

We visited your gravesite today to drop off new flowers. I know you're not there, but I don't ever want you to think we've forgotten you.

I miss you.

I started a new job this week. When I got the call and the job offer, I was so excited that I picked my phone up to text you. In that moment I forgot I lost you.

I miss you.

I always watched others lose people they loved. I tried to comfort them. I felt like I knew how hard it must be for them.

Then I lost you. I felt something deeper and more painful than anything I'd ever imagined.

They tell me it'll get easier.
They say it was all part of God's plan.
They ask me when I will move on.
They start sentences with, "Well at least...."
They tell me you're in a better place.

And every time someone tells me one of those sentences, it's like I just lost you all over again. Those words don't help.

But in loss, I found something, too.

I found that even though the pain never goes away, I can still find joy in moments.

I found moments to remind people of how loved they are while they are still here.

I found that sharing you and your story with others can help your memory live on and bring others together.

I found that when I allow others in, it helps me heal, too.

I found a faith that doesn't understand how or why loss happens, but can comfort me through the loss if I allow it.

Even in all that I've found, I still miss you. And that's ok.

BREATHE

Breathe in the peace you have earned.
Breathe out guilt that creeps in.

Breathe in Sunday mornings.
Breathe out the Sunday scaries.

Breathe in the joy that seems fleeting.
Breathe out the shame that lurks below.

Breathe in calm.
Breathe out chaos.

Breathe in the justice that needs to be released.
Breathe out the chaos that surrounds.

Breathe in the beauty that belongs in your daily frame.
Breath out the frustrations that fail to get the memo that it is
unwelcomed.

Breathe in faith.
Breathe out fear.

Breathe in _____
Breathe out _____

Inhale

FRUSTRATED

I don't know why I am, but I am.
I have yet to find a good reason, but sometimes you can't help the way you feel and today I am frustrated.

Last night, I went to bed in a perfectly good mood, but this morning my bones were tight, my thoughts were scattered, and agitation quickly found itself crawling under my skin.
Perhaps it's because I looked at my phone first thing this morning and started my day with comparison and skin care ads and photos of families who seem to have it all together.

I don't have it all together.
Maybe it's because nothing seems to fit right anymore, and the mirror reflects someone I no longer recognize.

Maybe it's because there are countless things to be thankful for, but today I am far from thankful and I know I should be.

Maybe it's the mountains I've built in my mind and I am tired of the arduous climb.
Maybe it's because I spilled my coffee.

Again.

Maybe I'm frustrated because life isn't going the way I thought it would or should.

I don't know why I am, but I am.

I'm still learning what to do with the frustration I feel.

For now, I'll leave it here.

ajdkajd gjcad merhp aesadhf jadn avadvjanb aafjhasdfn a jsdas rhntr nviu23iwn sjdf

There.

That's better.

HELLO. GOODBYE.

Hi.

Bye.

Two of the first few words taught early when our children begin to utter sounds.

Words that are easy to mimic, to remember, to recite.

And yet, these words, so simple, so easily released from our lips, hold special significance when greeting and when parting.

The first hello, the first hi. When meeting a new friend, a friend's child, a potential "friend-to-be-possibly-more-than-friend." Hi, hello, *maybe* hieeeee. The first impression. The greeting that initiates acknowledgement, a reunion, or a beginning. Hello.

I like hellos. Or at least most hellos. True, there are some hellos that are rife with weight, but hello can also be a choice to engage in. We don't always *have* to reciprocate a greeting back, nor initiate; but, in essence, it's polite, it's cordial, it's an invitation. Hello.

And then there are the good-byes. Some are abrupt, some are unsaid, some can't be said.

There are those who come into our lives at a certain time in their journey within our synchronized paths, who require a parting. A goodbye. Sometimes these partings have been years in the making, a soft and gradual fading, no feelings hurt, no emotional baggage attached…a quiet goodbye.

And then there are other partings that are more abrupt, jagged, ripping, painful.

A cancer that went undetected and now a few months, weeks remaining to spend with loved ones.

A relationship that once was functional, suddenly discovered to be toxic, requiring an end.

Friendships in which on one end, perceived safety, but on the other, an act of a betrayal of trust and loyalty–necessitating a solid, definitive goodbye.

Time is confusing. Some pains and memories fade over time, while other pains and memories resurrect with vengeance over time. The power, sheer ability, and willingness to heal from hurt, from pain, I find, to be possible through supernatural intervention…or a good laugh with friends who remind us that while some goodbyes are necessary, we are still loved.

We are valuable.

YOU are valuable.

So keep those hellos warm and near to yourself on a daily basis.

Good morning.

Hello.

How are you?

I'm…

Well.

Take care.

Good-bye.

CHOICE

Choice. Voice.
Two words that ring in my mind when it comes to making decisions
for the short term,
For the long term.

To know that I have a choice,
To remember that I have a voice.

Often, we are presented with the question:
What should I do?
Do I choose A, or do I choose B?

And there is always risk.
There's a risk to choose, there's the risk to NOT choose and never
know, or answer the perpetual gnawing of "What if..."

William Ernest Henley's "Invictus" echoes these infamous lines:
It matters not how strait the gate,
    How charged with punishments the scroll,
I am the master of my fate,
    I am the captain of my soul.

The best choices we make are made with the information we know at
the time,
and provokes a charge of action or inaction.
We muster the courage within us to choose–
Yes
Wait
or, No.

Any choice.
The choice to change and shift.
The choice to activate.
The choice to turn, go back.
The choice to leave.
The choice to stay.
So many choices that often come with so many voices.

But the choice and the power of choice resides within you, making the
best decision you can, with the information you have.

May wisdom be ever present so that we continue to make choices, big
and small, to lead us to the place of peace.

TENDERHEARTED

Tenderhearted.
That's how I want to live.
Gentle and kind with an open mind.
A mouth that is slow to speak and ears that are quick to listen.
Feet that move me toward the hurting and rest in the presence of the lonely.
Hands you can hold
and hands strong enough to hold two things at once.
Like,
Joy and sorrow.
Heavy and light.
Healing and wholeness.
What was and what will be.
Love and pain.
Tuesdays and Saturdays.
Tenderhearted.
That's how I want to live.

SERVICE

What does service look like to you?

Is it when we show up, willingly?

Listen attentively?

Practice proactive problem solving for others?

Thinking about how you can help without being asked?

Give without worrying about getting?

But...

Is service a gift, a responsibility, or both?

What happens when servanthood doesn't come naturally to a person?

What happens if service to others is not really second nature?

How do we release the people in our lives who love us but just aren't hard wired to be helpful?

Where does the balance for that lay?

HELLO

Hello,

I'm not sure how today finds you or where it finds you, but I'd like to offer a few reminders:

There is air in your lungs and a beat in your heart.

You are not your past nor is your profession your identity.

Grace is for you. It has always been for you. And it will be for you tomorrow, too.

You are allowed to slow down and rest and not look at your phone.

Keep hope close.

Remember how far you have come because you have come a long way.

Just because your life doesn't look like their life doesn't mean you are less or wrong or unworthy.

And when the lies get loud and the fear sets in remember this:

You are seen.

You are loved.

There is more to your story.

About the Authors

Dr. Alice Lee believes in activating and transforming students through education and literacy so that they are empowered to create a kinder and just world. She is the proud principal of Richmond Street School as well as the Director for Race, Equity, and Inclusion and Distance Learning for the El Segundo Unified School District. She has served as an assistant principal, teacher, instructional coach, professional developer, and taught abroad in Korea and Thailand. Dr. Lee has presented at conferences around the country including Get Your Lead On, League of Innovative Schools, Scholastic Reading Summits, UCLA's Graduate School of Education, and in Seoul, South Korea. She has participated and led webinars on the edWeb professional learning network, serving a global and digital educational community. She is a Principal Consultant for Bookelicious and served on Scholastic's Principal Advisory Board. Dr. Alice Lee is a three-time UCLA graduate and completed her doctorate in educational leadership with her dissertation focused on exploring lesson study as an improvement strategy for high-stakes accountability schools, students, and teachers. She has an Ed.D. in educational leadership, M.Ed. in elementary education, and administrative credential. She recently has been awarded Elementary Principal of the Year for the Association of California School Administrators (ACSA) Region 14.

Dr. Alice Lee is a first generation Korean-American. She lives in Los Angeles with her husband and two beautiful children. She is an avid reader of children's literature and passionate about sharing the love of literacy with families, teachers, and children. Connect with Alice on Twitter @dralicetlee.

Todd **Nesloney** is the Director of Culture and Strategic Leadership for the Texas Elementary Principals and Supervisors Association (TEPSA). He has also served as an award-winning principal of a PreK-5th Grade campus of over 775 students in a rural town in Texas. He has been recognized by the White House, John

C Maxwell, the Center for Digital Education, National School Board Association, the BAMMYS, and more for his work in education and with children. Todd has written four books, including *Kids Deserve It*, *Stories From Webb*, *Sparks in the Dark*, and *When Kids Lead*. He also released his first children's book *Spruce And Lucy*. He is very active on social media under the moniker Tech Ninja Todd. He is passionate about doing whatever it takes for our students and helping others tell their story. He lives in Brenham, Texas with his wife Lissette and their twin boys Liam and Brixton. Connect with Todd on his website at www.toddnesloney.com

Tanner Olson is an author, poet, podcaster, and speaker living in Nashville, Tennessee with his wife Sarah and their dog, Pancake. Tanner started writing in 2013 and began sharing his work under the name Written to Speak (@writtentospeak). The mission of Tanner's writing is to spread hope and announce love through written and spoken word poetry.

From classrooms to churches to organizations to coffee shops, Tanner has traveled across the country performing poetry, delivering messages of hope, and sharing stories.

He is the author of *I'm All Over the Place: A Book of Poems, Prayers, and Wonderings, As You Go: Words for the Unknown,* and *Walk A Little Slower.*

Connect with Tanner at writtentospeak.com or on Instagram and Twitter @writtentospeak

LaNesha Tabb is an apron-donning educator from Indianapolis, Indiana, with fifteen years of teaching and professional development experience. LaNesha is the content creator behind *Education With An Apron* where she creates fresh and innovative teaching resources. What exactly is *Education With An Apron?* It is a collection of teaching resources, courses, and professional development, specifically in writing and social studies from a primary educator. LaNesha's content is geared towards teachers who desire to think out of the box through rigorous and globally-connected resources, books, and ideas. LaNesha has worked with thousands of educators across the United

States through conferences and custom professional development sessions. LaNesha specializes in helping primary educators master their writing block time and teaching culturally relevant social studies topics. Connect with LaNesha on social media: apron_education and at laneshatabb.com

Omar Lopez has been an educator for 19 years. He taught English language arts and reading, science, and technology applications at a middle school in South Texas. Working with students along the US - Mexico border prompted him to look for ways to help his students capture the most out of a lesson. As a former English learner, he relied on illustrating his way into acquiring the language by sketching his own visual dictionary. As a teacher he used sketchnoting to help his students visualize concepts and deepen their understanding, especially for those acquiring English as a second language. He lives in the Rio Grande Valley with Fely, his wife of 21 years, and their two boys, Omar and Fer.

More from ConnectEDD Publishing

Since 2015, ConnectEDD has worked to transform education by empowering educators to become better-equipped to teach, learn, and lead. What started as a small company designed to provide professional learning events for educators has grown to include a variety of services to help teachers and administrators address essential challenges. ConnectEDD offers instructional and leadership coaching, professional development workshops focusing on a variety of educational topics, a roster of nationally recognized educator associates who possess hands-on knowledge and experience, educational conferences custom-designed to meet the specific needs of schools, districts, and state/national organizations, and ongoing, personalized support, both virtually and onsite. In 2020, ConnectEDD expanded to include publishing services designed to provide busy educators with books and resources consisting of practical information on a wide variety of teaching, learning, and leadership topics. Please visit us online at connecteddpublishing.com or contact us at: info@connecteddpublishing.com

Recent Publications:

Live Your Excellence: Action Guide by Jimmy Casas

Culturize: Action Guide by Jimmy Casas

Daily Inspiration for Educators: Positive Thoughts for Every Day of the Year by Jimmy Casas

Eyes on Culture: Multiply Excellence in Your School by Emily Paschall

Pause. Breathe. Flourish. Living Your Best Life as an Educator by William D. Parker

L.E.A.R.N.E.R. Finding the True, Good, and Beautiful in Education by Marita Diffenbaugh

Educator Reflection Tips Volume II: Refining Our Practice by Jami Fowler-White

Handle With Care: Managing Difficult Situations in Schools with Dignity and Respect by Jimmy Casas and Joy Kelly

Disruptive Thinking: Preparing Learners for Their Future by Eric Sheninger

Permission to be Great: Increasing Engagement in Your School by Dan Butler

Daily Inspiration for Educators: Positive Thoughts for Every Day of the Year, Volume II by Jimmy Casas

The 6 Literacy Levers: Creating a Community of Readers by Brad Gustafson

The Educator's ATLAS: Your Roadmap to Engagement by Weston Kieschnick